This little book is dedicated to you, a talisman to protect it.

Birth Of Evil

Down The Hatch

Look Ma, No Hands

Evil Genie

Straight For The Jugular

Spit It Out

It's Outside The Window

Waves Of Pain

Creepy Corridor

Cold Day In Hell

Lost In The Maze

Split Personality

Open Casket

The Gods Are Angry

Cannibal Dessert

Addicted To Pain

Tree Of Evil

Medusa's Pet

Deadly Passion

Headless Stampede

Devil's Chalice

My Cauldron Runneth Over

Hatchet To The Head

Blood Rising

Spike Collar

Parasite Within

No Bark All Bite

Acid Bath

It's Only A Virus

Hooded Stranger

Long Strange Drip

I Killed This For You

Uncontrollable Swelling

It's Going To Burst

Instrument Of Death

By The Light Of The Moon

Ancient Potion

The Door Down The Hall

Skeleton Key

Eyes Of The Spider

Conjoined Mess

Sacrificial Altar

Hidden In Plain Sight

Covered In Boils

Bloody Pulp

Burrowing Deeper

Creeping Tentacles

Drill Sergeant

Hammer Head

Claw Your Way Out

Morgue Trash

Gagged With Barbed Wire

Peculiar Plants

Smoking Gun

Stop Squirming

I See Right Through You

Watching From The Corner

Candlelight Sinner

Broken Veins

Forceful Blow

Trophy Wall

Alien Dissection

Under Pressure

Vampire Bats

What's In The Oven

He Didn't Make It

Meat Grinder

Behind The Mask

Ear Ache

Wicked Elf

Haunted Playground

Cocoon Is Opening

Fear The Reaper

While You Slept

Grim Tarot Card

Culinary Fright

Fruit Of Doom

End Of The Line

Manufactured by Amazon.ca
Bolton, ON